SPANISH-ENGLISH
Picture Dictionary

head
la cabeza

socks
los calcetines

bed
la cama

sailboat
el velero

tree
el árbol

tiger
el tigre

ball
la pelota

cake
la torta

truck
el camión

Over 350 words • Over 35 themes

First edition for the United States, its Dependencies, Canada, and the Philippines
published in 2011 by Barron's Educational Series, Inc.
© Copyright 2011 by b small publishing, Kingston-upon-Thames, UK.

All inquiries should be addressed to:
Barron's Educational Series, Inc.
250 Wireless Boulevard
Hauppauge, New York 11788
www.barronseduc.com

ISBN: 978-0-7641-4661-9
Library of Congress Control Number: 2010939981

Date of Manufacture: March 2013
Manufactured by: WKT, Shenzhen, Guangdong, China

Printed in China
9 8 7

The alphabet – El alfabeto

A a	ah		**N n**	EH-neh
B b	beh		**O o**	oh
C c	seh		**P p**	peh
D d	deh		**Q q**	coo
E e	eh		**R r**	EH-reh
F f	EH-feh		**S s**	EH-seh
G g	heh		**T t**	teh
H h	AH-cheh		**U u**	oo
I i	ee		**V v**	veh
J j	HOH-tah		**W w**	DOH-bleh veh
K k	kah		**X x**	EH-kees
L l	EH-leh		**Y y**	ee-gree-EH-gah
M m	EH-meh		**Z z**	SEH-tah

SPANISH-ENGLISH
Picture Dictionary

Catherine Bruzzone and Louise Millar

Illustrations by Louise Comfort and Steph Dix
Spanish adviser: Diego Blasco Vázquez

BARRON'S

1 one
uno/una
OO-noh/OO-nah

2 two
dos
dohs

3 three
tres
trehs

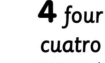
4 four
cuatro
KWAH-troh

5 five
cinco
SEEN-koh

6 six
seis
sayss

7 seven
siete
see-EH-teh

8 eight
ocho
OH-choh

9 nine
nueve
noo-EH-veh

10 ten
diez
dee-EHS

11
eleven
once
ON-seh

12
twelve
doce
DOH-seh

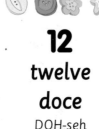
13
thirteen
trece
TREH-seh

14
fourteen
catorce
kah-TOHR-seh

15
fifteen
quince
KEEN-seh

16
sixteen
dieciséis
dee-eh-see-SAYSS

17
seventeen
diecisiete
dee-eh-see-see-EH-teh

18
eighteen
dieciocho
dee-eh-see-OH-choh

19
nineteen
diecinueve
dee-eh-see-noo-EH-veh

20
twenty
veinte
VEH-een-teh

Contents – Índice

EEN-dee-seh

The body – El cuerpo

ehl koo-EHR-poh

head
la cabeza
lah kah-BEH-sah

eyes
los ojos
lohs OH-hos

nose
la nariz
lah nah-REES

mouth
la boca
lah BOH-kah

shoulders
los hombros
lohs OHM-brohs

arm
el brazo
ehl BRAH-soh

hand
la mano
lah MAH-noh

leg
la pierna
lah pee-EHR-nah

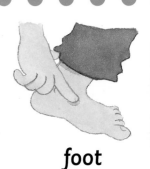

foot
el pie
ehl pee-EH

4

Clothes – La ropa

lah ROH-pah

skirt
la falda

lah FAHL-dah

dress
el vestido

ehl vehs-TEE-doh

pants
el pantalón

ehl pahn-tah-LOHN

coat
el abrigo

ehl ah-BREE-goh

shirt
la camisa

lah kah-MEE-sah

pajamas
el pijama

ehl pee-HAH-mah

shoes
los zapatos

lohs sah-PAH-tohs

socks
los calcetines

lohs kahl-see-TEE-nehs

hat
el sombrero

ehl sohm-BREH-roh

5

The family – La familia

mother/Mom
la madre/mamá
lah MAH-dreh/mah-MAH

father/Dad
el padre/papá
ehl PAH-dreh/pah-PAH

sister
la hermana
lah ehr-MAH-nah

brother
el hermano
ehl ehr-MAH-noh

grandmother
la abuela
lah ah-BWEH-lah

grandfather
el abuelo
ehl ah-BWEH-loh

aunt
la tía
lah TEE-ah

uncle
el tío
ehl TEE-oh

cousins
los primos
lohs PREE-mohs

6

The house – La casa

lah KAH-sah

kitchen
la cocina
lah koh-SEE-nah

living room
el salón
ehl sah-LOHN

bedroom
el dormitorio
ehl-dohr-mee-TOH-ree-oh

bathroom
l cuarto de baño
KWAHR-toh deh BAHN-yoh

toilet
el retrete
ehl reh-TREH-teh

stairs
las escaleras
lahs ehs-kah-LEH-rahs

floor
el piso
ehl PEE-soh

ceiling
el techo
ehl TEH-choh

garden
el jardín
ehl hahr-DEEN

7

In the house – En la casa
ehn lah KAH-sah

sofa
el sofá
ehl soh-FAH

armchair
el sillón
ehl see-YOHN

cushion
el cojín
ehl koh-HEEN

curtains
las cortinas
lahs kohr-TEE-nahs

picture
el cuadro
ehl KWAH-droh

stool
el taburete
ehl tah-boo-REH-teh

telephone
el teléfono
ehl teh-LEH-foh-noh

computer
la computadora
lah kohm-poo-tah-DOH-rah

television
el televisor
ehl teh-leh-vee-SOHR

8

The kitchen – La cocina
lah koh-SEE-nah

sink
el fregadero
ehl freh-gah-DEH-roh

refrigerator
el refrigerador
ehl reh-free-heh-rah-DOHR

stove
la cocina
lah koh-SEE-nah

knife
el cuchillo
ehl koo-CHEE-yoh

spoon
la cuchara
lah koo-CHAH-rah

fork
el tenedor
ehl teh-neh-DOHR

plate
el plato
ehl PLAH-toh

glass
el vaso
ehl VAH-soh

pot
la cacerola
lah kah-seh-ROH-lah

9

The bedroom – El dormitorio

ehl dohr-mee-TOH-ree-oh

bed
la cama
lah KAH-mah

chest of drawers
la cómoda
lah KOH-moh-dah

wardrobe
el armario
ehl ahr-MAH-ree-oh

alarm clock
el despertador
ehl dehs-pehr-tah-DOHR

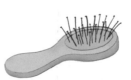

hairbrush
el cepillo del pelo
ehl seh-PEE-yoh dehl PEH-loh

shelf
el estante
ehl ehs-TAHN-teh

rug
la alfombra
lah ahl-FOHM-brah

window
la ventana
lah vehn-TAH-nah

door
la puerta
lah PWEHR-tah

The bathroom – El cuarto de baño
ehl KWAHR-toh deh BAHN-yoh

washbowl
el lavamanos
ehl lah-vah-MAH-nohs

toilet
el retrete
ehl reh-TREH-teh

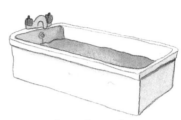

bathtub
la bañera
lah bahn-YEH-rah

shower
la ducha
lah DOO-chah

mirror
el espejo
ehl ehs-PEH-hoh

towel
la toalla
lah toh-AH-yah

toothpaste
pasta de dientes
AHS-tah deh dee-EHN-tehs

toothbrush
el cepillo de dientes
ehl seh-PEE-yoh deh ee-EHN-tehs

soap
el jabón
ehl hah-BOHN

11

The city – La ciudad

lah see-oo-DAHD

house
la casa
lah KAH-sah

school
la escuela
lah ehs-KWEH-lah

station
la estación
lah ehs-tah-see-OHN

shop
la tienda
lah tee-EHN-dah

post office
la oficina de correos
lah oh-fee-SEE-nah deh
kohr-REH-ohs

supermarket
el supermercad
ehl soo-pehr-mehr-KAH-c

factory
la fábrica
lah FAH-bree-kah

market
el mercado
ehl mehr-KAH-doh

cinema
el cine
ehl SEE-neh

The street – La calle

lah KAH-yeh

street
la calle

lah KAH-yeh

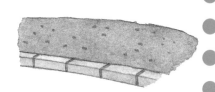

sidewalk
la acera

lah ah-SEH-rah

bus stop
la parada

lah pah-RAH-dah

traffic light
el semáforo

ehl seh-MAH-foh-roh

roundabout
la rotonda

lah roh-TOHN-dah

streetlight
la farola

lah fah-ROH-lah

road sign
señal de tráfico

ehn-YAHL deh TRAH-fee-koh

zebra crossing
el paso de cebra

ehl PAH-soh deh SEH-brah

police officer
el policía

ehl poh-lee-SEE-ah 13

Vehicles – Los vehículos

lohs veh-EE-koo-lohs

bus
el autobús
ehl aw-toh-BOOS

ambulance
la ambulancia
lah ahm-boo-LAHN-see-ah

bicycle
la bicicleta
lah bee-see-KLEH-tah

car
el coche
ehl KOH-cheh

police car
el coche de policía
ehl KOH-cheh deh poh-lee-SEE-ah

motorcycle
la motocicleta
lah moh-toh-see-KLEH-t

truck
el camión
14 ehl kah-mee-OHN

fire engine
el camión de bomberos
ehl kah-mee-OHN deh bohm-BEH-rohs

van
la furgoneta
lah foor-goh-NEH-tah

The park – El parque

ehl PAHR-keh

path
el camino
ehl kah-MEE-noh

seesaw
el balancín
ehl bah-lahn-SEEN

swing
el columpio
ehl koh-LOOM-pee-oh

girl
la niña
lah NEEN-yah

boy
el niño
ehl NEEN-yoh

child
el niño/la niña
ehl NEEN-yoh/lah NEEN-yah

lake
el lago
ehl LAH-goh

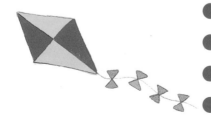

kite
la cometa
lah koh-MEH-tah

bench
el banco
ehl BAHN-koh

15

The hospital – El hospital

ehl ohs-pee-TAHL

doctor
la doctora
lah dohk-TOH-rah

nurse
el enfermero
ehl ehn-fehr-MEH-roh

x-ray
la radiografía
lah rah-dee-oh-grah-FEE-

thermometer
el termómetro
ehl tehr-MOH-meh-troh

medicine
la medicina
lah meh-dee-SEE-nah

bandage
el vendaje
ehl vehn-DAH-heh

cast
la escayola
lah ehs-kah-YOH-lah

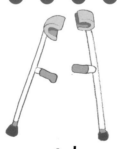

crutches
las muletas
lahs moo-LEH-tahs

wheelchair
la silla de rueda
lah SEE-yah deh RWEH-d

The supermarket – El supermercado

egg
el huevo

ehl HWEH-voh

bread
el pan

ehl pahn

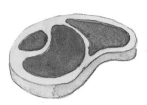

meat
la carne

lah KAHR-neh

rice
el arroz

ehl ahr-ROHS

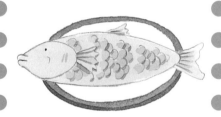

fish
el pescado

ehl pehs-KAH-doh

butter
la mantequilla

lah mahn-teh-KEE-yah

milk
la leche

lah LEH-cheh

pasta
la pasta

lah PAHS-tah

sugar
el azúcar

ehl ah-SOO-kahr

Fruit – La fruta
lah FROO-tah

apple
la manzana
lah mahn-SAH-nah

peach
el melocotón
ehl meh-loh-koh-TOHN

cherry
la cereza
lah seh-REH-sah

orange
la naranja
lah nah-RAHN-hah

pineapple
la piña
lah PEEN-yah

mango
el mango
ehl MAHN-goh

banana
el plátano
ehl PLAH-tah-noh

grapes
las uvas
lahs OO-vahs

strawberry
la fresa
lah FREH-sah

Vegetables – Las verduras

lahs vehr-DOO-rahs

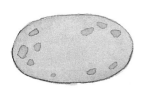

potato
la papa
lah PAH-pah

corn
el maíz
ehl mah-EES

cabbage
la col
lah kohl

zucchini
el calabacín
ehl kah-lah-bah-SEEN

carrot
la zanahoria
lah sah-nah-OH-ree-ah

eggplant
la berenjena
lah beh-rehn-HEH-nah

tomato
el tomate
ehl toh-MAH-teh

lettuce
la lechuga
lah leh-CHOO-gah

celery
el apio
ehl AH-pee-oh

The country- El campo

tree
el árbol

ehl AHR-bohl

grass
la hierba

lah ee-EHR-bah

flower
la flor

lah flohr

field
el prado

ehl PRAH-doh

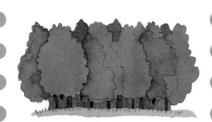

forest
el bosque

ehl BOHS-keh

mountain
la montaña

lah mohn-TAHN-yah

bridge
el puente

ehl PWEHN-teh

river
el río

ehl REE-oh

bird
el pájaro

ehl PAH-hah-roh

20

In the forest – En el bosque
ehn ehl BOHS-keh

fox
el zorro
ehl SOHR-roh

squirrel
la ardilla
lah ahr-DEE-yah

deer
el ciervo
ehl see-EHR-voh

rabbit
el conejo
ehl koh-NEH-hoh

brown bear
el oso marrón
ehl OH-soh mahr-ROHN

butterfly
la mariposa
lah mah-ree-POH-sah

beetle
el escarabajo
hl ehs-kah-rah-BAH-hoh

caterpillar
la oruga
lah oh-ROO-gah

fly
la mosca
lah MOHS-kah

21

The farm – La granja
lah GRAHN-hah

cat
el gato
ehl GAH-toh

mouse
el ratón
ehl rah-TOHN

dog
el perro
ehl PEHR-roh

cow
la vaca
lah VAH-kah

horse
el caballo
ehl kah-BAH-yoh

pig
el cerdo
ehl SEHR-doh

sheep
la oveja
lah oh-VEH-hah

duck
el pato
ehl PAH-toh

goat
la cabra
lah KAH-brah

Baby animals – Las crías de animales

lahs KREE-ahs deh ah-nee-MAH-lehs

puppy
el cachorro
ehl kah-CHOHR-roh

kitten
el gatito
ehl gah-TEE-toh

foal
el potro
ehl POH-troh

calf
el ternero
ehl tehr-NEH-roh

chick
el pollito
ehl poh-YEE-toh

cygnet
el pichón de cisne
ehl pee-CHOHN deh SEES-neh

duckling
el patito
ehl pah-TEE-toh

lamb
el cordero
ehl kohr-DEH-roh

piglet
el cerdito
ehl sehr-DEE-toh

23

At the beach – En la playa

ehn lah PLAH-yah

sea
el mar
ehl mahr

seagull
la gaviota
lah gah-vee-OH-tah

sand
la arena
lah ah-REH-nah

fish
el pez
ehl pehs

seaweed
el alga marina
ehl AHL-gah mah-REE-nah

shell
la concha
lah KOHN-chah

rock
la roca
lah ROH-kah

sailboat
el velero
ehl veh-LEH-roh

wave
la ola
lah OH-lah

24

Under the sea – Bajo el mar

BAH-oh ehl mahr

octopus
el pulpo
ehl POOL-poh

starfish
la estrella de mar
lah ehs-TREH-yah deh mahr

jellyfish
la medusa
lah meh-DOO-sah

lobster
la langosta
lah lahn-GOHS-tah

shark
el tiburón
ehl tee-boo-ROHN

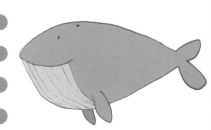

whale
la ballena
lah bah-YEH-nah

wreck
el naufragio
hl nah-oo-FRAH-hee-oh

diver
el buceador
ehl boo-seh-ah-DOHR

coral
el coral
ehl koh-RAHL

The zoo – El zoológico

ehl soh-oh-LOH-hee-koh

giraffe
la jirafa
lah hee-RAH-fah

snake
la serpiente
lah sehr-pee-EHN-teh

hippopotamus
el hipopótamo
ehl ee-poh-POH-tah-mo

dolphin
el delfín
ehl dehl-FEEN

tiger
el tigre
ehl TEE-greh

crocodile
el cocodrilo
ehl koh-koh-DREE-loh

polar bear
el oso polar
26 ehl OH-soh poh-LAHR

lion
el león
ehl leh-OHN

elephant
el elefante
ehl eh-leh-FAHN-teh

Toys – Los juguetes

los hoo-GEH-tehs

teddy bear
el osito

ehl oh-SEE-toh

robot
el robot

ehl roh-BOHT

ball
la pelota

lah peh-LOH-tah

puzzle
el rompecabezas

l rohm-peh-kah-BEH-sahs

toy train
el trencito de juguete

ehl trehn-SEE-toh deh hoo-GEH-teh

game
el juego

ehl HWEH-goh

doll
la muñeca

lah moon-YEH-kah

paints
las pinturas

lahs peen-TOO-rahs

drum
el tambor

ehl tahm-BOHR

27

Party time! – ¡Fiesta!

fee-EHS-tah

sandwich
el bocadillo

ehl boh-kah-DEE-yoh

chocolate
el chocolate

ehl choh-koh-LAH-teh

french fries
las papas fritas

lahs PAH-pahs FREE-tah

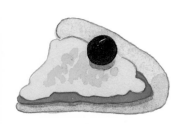

pizza
la pizza

lah PEE-tsah

cake
la torta

lah TOHR-tah

ice cream
el helado

ehl eh-LAH-doh

cola
el refresco

ehl reh-FREHS-koh

orange juice
el jugo de naranja

ehl HOO-goh deh nah-RAHN-hah

water
el agua

ehl AH-gwah

28

The classroom – La clase

lah KLAH-seh

teacher
la profesora

lah proh-feh-SOH-rah

table
la mesa

lah MEH-sah

chair
la silla

lah SEE-yah

book
el libro

ehl LEE-broh

color pencil
el lápiz de color

ehl LAH-pees deh koh-LOHR

glue
el pegamento

ehl peh-gah-MEHN-toh

paper
el papel

ehl pah-PEHL

pen
la pluma

lah PLOO-mah

scissors
las tijeras

lahs tee-HEH-rahs **29**

Sports - Los deportes

soccer
el fútbol
ehl FOOT-bohl

table tennis
el ping pong
ehl peeng pohng

skiing
el esquí
ehl ehs-KEY

gymnastics
la gimnasia
lah heem-NAH-see-ah

cycling
el ciclismo
ehl see-KLEES-moh

athletics
el atletismo
ehl aht-leh-TEES-moh

fishing
la pesca
lah PEHS-kah

swimming
la natación
lah nah-tah-see-OHN

basketball
el baloncesto
ehl bah-lohn-SEHS-toh

30

Weather – El tiempo

ehl tee-EHM-poh

sun
el sol
ehl sohl

heat
el calor
ehl kah-LOHR

rain
la lluvia
lah YOO-vee-ah

cloud
la nube
lah NOO-beh

wind
el viento
ehl vee-EHN-toh

storm
la tormenta
lah tohr-MEHN-tah

fog
la niebla
lah nee-EH-blah

cold
el frío
ehl FREE-oh

snow
la nieve
lah nee-EH-veh

31

Action words – Palabras de acción

pah-LAH-brahs deh ahk-see-OHN

to run
correr
kohr-REHR

to walk
andar
ahn-DAHR

to crawl
gatear
gah-teh-AHR

to carry
llevar
yeh-VAHR

to stand
estar de pie
ehs-TAHR deh pee-EH

to sit
estar sentado
ehs-TAHR sehn-TAH-doh

to push
empujar
ehm-poo-HAHR

to hug
abrazar
ah-brah-SAHR

to pull
halar
hah-LAHR

32

Storybooks – Los libros de cuentos

lohs LEE-brohs deh KWEHN-tohs

dragon
el dragón

ehl drah-GOHN

mermaid
la sirena

lah see-REH-nah

knight
el caballero

ehl kah-bah-YEH-roh

pirate
el pirata

ehl pee-RAH-tah

fairy
el hada

ehl AH-dah

witch
la bruja

lah BROO-hah

prince
el príncipe

ehl PREEN-see-peh

princess
la princesa

lah preen-SEH-sah

castle
el castillo

ehl kahs-TEE-yoh

The building site – La obra

lah OH-brah

digger
la excavadora

lah ex-kah-vah-DOH-rah

cement mixer
el camión hormigonera

ehl kah-mee-OHN
ohr-mee-goh-NEH-rah

crane
la grúa

lah GROO-ah

scaffolding
el andamio

ehl ahn-DAH-mee-oh

dump truck
el camión volquete

ehl kah-mee-OHN vohl-KEH-teh

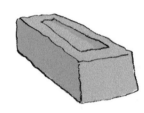

brick
el ladrillo

ehl lah-DREE-yoh

bulldozer
el bulldozer

ehl bool-DOH-zehr

ladder
la escalera

lah ehs-kah-LEH-rah

wood
el tablón

ehl tah-BLOHN

Tools – Las herramientas

lahs ehr-rah-mee-EHN-tahs

rake
el rastrillo

ehl rahs-TREE-yoh

shovel
la pala

lah PAH-lah

bucket
el cubo

ehl KOO-boh

wheelbarrow
la carretilla

lah kahr-reh-TEE-yah

hammer
el martillo

ehl mahr-TEE-yoh

nail
el clavo

ehl KLAH-voh

saw
el serrucho

ehl sehr-ROO-choh

hose
la manguera

lah mahn-GEH-rah

paintbrush
la brocha

lah BROH-chah

35

Luggage – El equipaje
ehl eh-kee-PAH-heh

suitcase
la maleta
lah mah-LEH-tah

schoolbag
el bolsón
ehl bohl-SOHN

trunk
el baúl
ehl bah-OOL

backpack
la mochila
lah moh-CHEE-lah

handbag
la cartera
lah kahr-TEH-rah

briefcase
el maletín
ehl mah-leh-TEEN

basket
la cesta
lah SEHS-tah

shopping bag
la bolsa de compras
lah BOHL-sah deh KOHM-prahs

purse
el monedero
ehl moh-neh-DEH-roh

36

Train travel – El viaje en tren

ehl vee-AH-heh ehn trehn

ticket
el billete

ehl bee-YEH-teh

conductor
el revisor

ehl reh-vee-SOHR

platform
el andén

ehl ahn-DEHN

engineer
la maquinista

lah mah-kee-NEES-tah

signal
la señal

lah sehn-YAHL

train
el tren

ehl trehn

seat
el asiento

ehl ah-see-EHN-toh

level crossing
el paso a nivel

ehl PAH-soh ah nee-VEHL

rails
los rieles

lohs ree-EH-lehs

Air travel – El viaje en avión

ehl vee-AH-heh ehn ah-vee-OHN

airplane
el avión

ehl ah-vee-OHN

airport
el aeropuerto

ehl ah-eh-roh-PWEHR-toh

pilot
el piloto

ehl pee-LOH-toh

flight attendant
la azafata

lah ah-sah-FAH-tah

x-ray machine
la máquina de rayos x

lah MAH-kee-nah
deh RAH-yohs EH-kees

passport
el pasaporte

ehl pah-sah-POHR-teh

hand truck
el carrito

ehl kahr-REE-toh

snack
el refrigerio

ehl reh-free-HEH-ree-oh

seatbelt
el cinturón de seguri

ehl seen-too-ROHN deh
seh-goo-ree-DAHD

At sea – En el mar

ehn ehl mahr

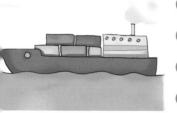

ship
el barco
ehl BAHR-koh

yacht
el yate
ehl YAH-teh

rowboat
el bote a remos
ehl BOH-teh ah REH-mohs

tanker
el petrolero
ehl peh-troh-LEH-roh

fishing boat
el barco de pesca
ehl BAHR-koh deh PEHS-kah

ferry
el ferry
ehl FEHR-ree

buoy
la boya
lay BOH-yah

port
el puerto
ehl PWEHR-toh

lighthouse
el faro
ehl FAH-roh

Opposites – Los contrarios

lohs kohn-TRAH-ree-ohs

friendly
amable
ah-MAH-bleh

angry
enojado/enojada
eh-noh-HAH-doh/eh-noh-HAH-dah

thin
delgado/delgad
dehl-GAH-doh/dehl-GAH-d

clean
limpio/limpia
LEEM-pee-oh/LEEM-pee-ah

dirty
sucio/sucia
SOO-see-oh/SOO-see-ah

neat
ordenado/ordena
ohr-deh-NAH-doh/ohr-deh-NAH

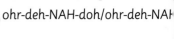

sad
triste
TREES-teh

happy
feliz
feh-LEES

heavy
pesado/pesada
peh-SAH-doh/peh-SAH-d

40

Opposites – Los contrarios
lohs kohn-TRAH-ree-ohs

fat
gordo/gorda
GOHR-doh/GOHR-dah

tall
alto/alta
AHL-toh/AHL-tah

short
bajo/baja
BAH-hoh/BAH-hah

messy
ordenado/desordenada
deh-sohr-deh-NAH-doh/
deh-sohr-deh-NAH-dah

fast
rápido/rápida
RAH-pee-doh/RAH-pee-dah

slow
lento/lenta
LEHN-toh/LEHN-tah

light
ligero/ligera
lee-HEH-roh/lee-HEH-rah

beautiful
hermoso/hermosa
ehr-MOH-soh/ehr-MOH-sah

ugly
feo/fea
FEH-oh/FEH-ah

41

Spanish/español – English/inglés

abrazar to hug
el abrigo coat
la abuela grandmother
el abuelo grandfather
la acera sidewalk
el aeropuerto airport
el agua water
la alfombra rug
el alga marina seaweed
alto/alta tall
amable friendly
amarillo/amarilla yellow
la ambulancia ambulance
el andamio scaffolding
andar to walk
el andén platform
el apio celery
el árbol tree
la ardilla squirrel
la arena sand
el armario wardrobe
el arroz rice
el asiento seat
el atletismo athletics
el autobús bus
el avión airplane
la azafata flight attendant
el azúcar sugar
azul blue
bajo/baja short
el balancín seesaw
la ballena whale
el baloncesto basketball
el banco bench
la bañera bathtub
el barco ship
el barco de pesca fishing boat
el baúl trunk
la berenjena eggplant
la bicicleta bicycle
el billete ticket

blanco/blanca white
la boca mouth
el bocadillo sandwich
la bolsa de compras shopping bag
el bolsón schoolbag
el bosque forest
el bote a remos rowboat
la boya buoy
el brazo arm
la brocha paintbrush
la bruja witch
el buceador diver
el bulldozer bulldozer
el caballero knight
el caballo horse
la cabeza head
la cabra goat
la cacerola pot
el cachorro puppy
el calabacín zucchini
los calcetines socks
la calle street
el calor heat
la cama bed
el camino path
el camión truck
el camión de bomberos fire engine
el camión hormigonera cement mixer
el camión volquete dump truck
la camisa shirt
el campo country
la carne meat
la carretilla wheelbarrow
la cartera handbag
el carrito hand truck
la casa house
el castillo castle
catorce fourteen
el cepillo de dientes toothbrush
el cepillo del pelo hairbrush
el cerdito piglet

el cerdo pig
la cereza cherry
la cesta basket
el chocolate chocolate
el ciclismo cycling
el ciervo deer
cinco five
el cine cinema
el cinturón de seguridad seatbelt
la ciudad city
la clase classroom
el clavo nail
el coche car
el coche de policía police car
la cocina kitchen, stove
el cocodrilo crocodile
el cojín cushion
la col cabbage
los colores colors
la cometa kite
la cómoda chest of drawers
la computadora computer
la concha shell
el conejo rabbit
el coral coral
el cordero lamb
correr to run
las cortinas curtains
el cuadro picture
el cuarto de baño bathroom
cuatro four
el cubo bucket
la cuchara spoon
el cuchillo knife
el cuerpo body
el delfín dolphin
delgado/delgada thin
los deportes sports
desordenado/desordenada messy
el despertador alarm clock
diecinueve nineteen
dieciocho eighteen

eciséis sixteen
ecisiete seventeen
ez ten
ce twelve
doctora doctor
dormitorio bedroom
s two
dragón dragon
ducha shower
elefante elephant
pujar to push
enfermero nurse
ojado/enojada angry
equipaje luggage
escalera ladder
s escaleras stairs
escarabajo beetle
escayola cast
escuela school
espejo mirror
esquí skiing
estación station
estante shelf
tar de pie to stand
tar sentado to sit
estrella de mar starfish
excavadora digger
fábrica factory
falda skirt
familia family
faro lighthouse
farola streetlight
iz happy
/fea ugly
ferry ferry
fiesta party
flor flower
fregadero sink
fresa strawberry
frío cold
fruta fruit
furgoneta van
fútbol soccer
tear to crawl
gatito kitten

el gato cat
la gaviota seagull
la gimnasia gymnastics
gordo/gorda fat
la granja farm
la grúa crane
el hada fairy
halar to pull
el helado ice cream
la hermana sister
el hermano brother
hermoso/hermosa beautiful
las herramientas tools
la hierba grass
el hipopótamo hippopotamus
los hombros shoulders
el hospital hospital
el huevo egg
el jabón soap
el jardín garden
la jirafa giraffe
el jugo de naranja orange juice
el juguete toy
el ladrillo brick
el lago lake
la langosta lobster
el lápiz de color color pencil
el lavamanos washbowl
la leche milk
la lechuga lettuce
lento/lenta slow
el león lion
el libro book
ligero/ligera light
limpio/limpia clean
llevar to carry
la lluvia rain
la madre mother
el maíz corn
la maleta suitcase
el maletín briefcase
mamá Mom
el mango mango
la manguera hose
la mano hand

la mantequilla butter
la manzana apple
la máquina de rayos x x-ray machine
la maquinista engineer
el mar sea
la mariposa butterfly
marrón brown
el martillo hammer
la matación swimming
la medicina medicine
la medusa jellyfish
el melocotón peach
el mercado market
la mesa table
la mochila backpack
el monedero purse
la montaña mountain
morado/morada purple
la mosca fly
la motocicleta motorcycle
las muletas crutches
la muñeca doll
la naranja orange (fruit)
naranja orange (color)
la nariz nose
la natación swimming
el naufragio wreck
negro/negra black
la niebla fog
la nieve snow
la niña girl
el niño boy
el niño/la niña child
la nube cloud
nueve nine
la obra building site
ocho eight
la oficina de correos post office
los ojos eyes
la ola wave
once eleven
ordenado/ordenada neat
la oruga caterpillar
el osito teddy bear

43

el oso marrón brown bear
el oso polar polar bear
la oveja sheep
el padre father
el pájaro bird
la pala shovel
el pan bread
el pantalón pants
papá Dad
la papa potato
las papas fritas french fries
el papel paper
la parada bus stop
el pasaporte passport
el paso a nivel level crossing
el paso de cebra zebra crossing
la pasta pasta
la pasta de dientes toothpaste
el patito duckling
el pato duck
el pegamento glue
la pelota ball
el perro dog
pesado/pesada heavy
el pescado fish (to eat)
la pesca fishing
el petrolero tanker
el pez fish (in the sea)
el pichón de cisne cygnet
el pie foot
la pierna leg
el pijama pajamas
el piloto pilot
la piña pineapple
el ping pong table tennis
las pinturas paints
el pirata pirate
el piso floor
la pizza pizza
el plátano banana
el plato plate
la playa beach
la pluma pen
el policía police officer

el pollito chick
el potro foal
el prado field
los primos cousins
la princesa princess
el príncipe prince
la profesora teacher
el puente bridge
la puerta door
el puerto port
el pulpo octopus
quince fifteen
la radiografía x-ray
rápido/rápida fast
el rastrillo rake
el ratón mouse
el refresco cola
el refrigerador refrigerator
el refrigerio snack
el retrete toilet
el revisor conductor
los rieles rails
el río river
el robot robot
la roca rock
rojo/roja red
el rompecabezas puzzle
la ropa clothes
la rotonda roundabout
el salón living room
seis six
el semáforo traffic light
la señal signal
la señal de tráfico road sign
la serpiente snake
el serrucho saw
siete seven
la silla chair
la silla de ruedas wheelchair
el sillón armchair
la sirena mermaid
el sofá sofa
el sol sun
el sombrero hat
sucio/sucia dirty

el supermercado supermarket
el tablón wood
el taburete stool
el tambor drum
el techo ceiling
el teléfono telephone
el televisor television
el tenedor fork
el termómetro thermometer
el ternero calf
la tía aunt
el tiburón shark
el tiempo weather
la tienda shop
el tigre tiger
las tijeras scissors
el tío uncle
la toalla towel
el tomate tomato
la tormenta storm
la torta cake
trece thirteen
el tren train
el trencito de juguete toy train
tres three
triste sad
uno/una one
las uvas grapes
la vaca cow
el vaso glass
los vehículos vehicles
veinte twenty
el velero sailboat
el vendaje bandage
la ventana window
verde green
las verduras vegetables
el vestido dress
el viaje travel
el viento wind
el yate yacht
la zanahoria carrot
los zapatos shoes
el zoológico zoo
el zorro fox

English/inglés – Spanish/español

airplane el avión	bus el autobús	crane la grúa
airport el aeropuerto	bus stop la parada	to crawl gatear
alarm clock el despertador	butter la mantequilla	crocodile el cocodrilo
ambulance la ambulancia	butterfly la mariposa	crutches las muletas
angry enojado/enojada	cabbage la col	curtains las cortinas
apple la manzana	cake la torta	cushion el cojín
arm el brazo	calf el ternero	cycling ciclismo
armchair el sillón	car el coche	cygnet el pichón de cisne
athletics el atletismo	carrot la zanahoria	Dad papá
aunt la tía	to carry llevar	deer el ciervo
backpack la mochila	cast la escayola	digger la excavadora
ball la pelota	castle el castillo	dirty sucio/sucia
banana el plátano	cat el gato	diver el buceador
bandage el vendaje	caterpillar la oruga	doctor la doctora
basket la cesta	ceiling el techo	dog el perro
basketball el baloncesto	celery el apio	doll la muñeca
bathroom el cuarto de baño	cement mixer	dolphin el delfín
bathtub la bañera	el camión hormigonera	door la puerta
beach la playa	chair la silla	dragon el dragón
beautiful hermoso/hermosa	cherry la cereza	dress el vestido
bed la cama	chest of drawers la cómoda	drum el tambor
bedroom el dormitorio	chick el pollito	duck el pato
beetle el escarabajo	child el niño/la niña	duckling el patito
bench el banco	chocolate el chocolate	dump truck el camión volquete
bicycle la bicicleta	cinema el cine	egg el huevo
bird el pájaro	city la ciudad	eggplant la berenjena
black negro/negra	classroom la clase	eight ocho
blue azul	clean limpio/limpia	eighteen dieciocho
body el cuerpo	clothes la ropa	elephant el elefante
book el libro	cloud la nube	eleven once
boy el niño	coat el abrigo	engineer la maquinista
bread el pan	cola el refresco	eyes los ojos
brick el ladrillo	cold el frío	factory la fábrica
bridge el puente	color pencil el lápiz de color	fairy el hada
briefcase el maletín	colors los colores	family la familia
brother el hermano	computer la computadora	farm la granja
brown marrón	conductor el revisor	fast rápido/rápida
brown bear el oso marrón	coral el coral	fat gordo/gorda
bucket el cubo	corn el maíz	father el padre
building site la obra	country el campo	ferry el ferry
bulldozer el bulldozer	cousins los primos	field el prado
buoy la boya	cow la vaca	fifteen quince

fire engine el camión de bomberos	**horse** el caballo	**one** uno/una
fish (to eat) el pescado	**hose** la manguera	**orange (fruit)** la naranja
fish (in the sea) el pez	**hospital** el hospital	**orange (color)** naranja
fishing la pesca	**house** la casa	**orange juice** el jugo de naranja
fishing boat el barco de pesca	**to hug** abrazar	**paintbrush** la brocha
five cinco	**ice cream** el helado	**paints** las pinturas
flight attendant la azafata	**jellyfish** la medusa	**pajamas** el pijama
floor el piso	**kitchen** la cocina	**pants** el pantalón
flower la flor	**kite** la cometa	**paper** el papel
fly la mosca	**kitten** el gatito	**party** la fiesta
foal el potro	**knife** el cuchillo	**passport** el pasaporte
fog la niebla	**knight** el caballero	**pasta** la pasta
foot el pie	**ladder** la escalera	**path** el camino
forest el bosque	**lake** el lago	**peach** el melocotón
fork el tenedor	**lamb** el cordero	**pen** la pluma
four cuatro	**leg** la pierna	**picture** el cuadro
fourteen catorce	**lettuce** la lechuga	**pig** el cerdo
fox el zorro	**level crossing** el paso a nivel	**piglet** el cerdito
french fries las papas fritas	**light** ligero/ligera	**pilot** el piloto
friendly amable	**lighthouse** el faro	**pineapple** la piña
fruit la fruta	**lion** el león	**pirate** el pirata
garden el jardín	**living room** el salón	**pizza** la pizza
giraffe la jirafa	**lobster** la langosta	**plate** el plato
girl la niña	**luggage** el equipaje	**platform** el andén
glass el vaso	**mango** el mango	**polar bear** el oso polar
glue el pegamento	**market** el mercado	**police car** el coche de policía
goat la cabra	**meat** la carne	**police officer** el policía
grandfather el abuelo	**medicine** la medicina	**port** el puerto
grandmother la abuela	**mermaid** la sirena	**post office** la oficina de correos
grapes las uvas	**messy** desordenado/desordenada	**pot** la cacerola
grass la hierba	**milk** la leche	**potato** la papa
green verde	**mirror** el espejo	**prince** el príncipe
gymnastics la gimnasia	**Mom** mamá	**princess** la princesa
hairbrush el cepillo del pelo	**mother** la madre	**to pull** halar
hammer el martillo	**motorcycle** la motocicleta	**puppy** el cachorro
hand la mano	**mountain** la montaña	**purple** morado/morada
handbag la cartera	**mouse** el ratón	**purse** el monedero
hand truck el carrito	**mouth** la boca	**to push** empujar
happy feliz	**nail** el clavo	**puzzle** el rompecabezas
hat el sombrero	**neat** ordenado/ordenada	**rabbit** el conejo
head la cabeza	**nine** nueve	**rails** los rieles
heat el calor	**nineteen** diecinueve	**rain** la lluvia
heavy pesado/pesada	**nose** la nariz	**rake** el rastrillo
hippopotamus el hipopótamo	**nurse** el enfermero	**red** rojo/roja
	octopus el pulpo	**refrigerator** el refrigerador

e	el arroz
er	el río
ad sign	la señal de tráfico
bot	el robot
ck	la roca
undabout	la rotonda
wboat	el bote a remos
g	la alfombra
run	correr
d	triste
ilboat	el velero
nd	la arena
ndwich	el bocadillo
w	el serrucho
affolding	el andamio
ool	la escuela
oolbag	el bolsón
ssors	las tijeras
a	el mar
agull	la gaviota
at	el asiento
atbelt	el cinturón de seguridad
aweed	el alga marina
esaw	el balancín
ven	siete
venteen	diecisiete
ark	el tiburón
eep	la oveja
elf	el estante
ell	la concha
ip	el barco
irt	la camisa
oes	los zapatos
op	la tienda
opping bag	la bolsa de compras
ort	bajo/baja
oulders	los hombros
ovel	la pala
ower	la ducha
dewalk	la acera
nal	la señal
k	el fregadero
ter	la hermana
sit	estar sentado
	seis

sixteen	dieciséis
skiing	el esquí
skirt	la falda
slow	lento/lenta
snack	el refrigerio
snake	la serpiente
snow	la nieve
soap	el jabón
soccer	el fútbol
socks	los calcetines
sofa	el sofá
spoon	la cuchara
sports	los deportes
squirrel	la ardilla
stairs	las escaleras
to stand	estar de pie
starfish	la estrella de mar
station	la estación
stool	el taburete
storm	la tormenta
stove	la cocina
strawberry	la fresa
street	la calle
streetlight	la farola
sugar	el azúcar
suitcase	la maleta
sun	el sol
supermarket	el supermercado
swimming	la natación
table	la mesa
table tennis	el ping pong
tall	alto/alta
tanker	el petrolero
teacher	la profesora
teddy bear	el osito
telephone	el teléfono
television	el televisor
ten	diez
thermometer	el termómetro
thin	delgado/delgada
thirteen	trece
three	tres
ticket	el billete
tiger	el tigre
toilet	el retrete

tomato	el tomate
tools	las herramientas
toothbrush	el cepillo de dientes
toothpaste	la pasta de dientes
towel	la toalla
toy	el juguete
toy train	el trencito de juguete
traffic light	el semáforo
train	el tren
travel	el viaje
tree	el árbol
truck	el camión
trunk	el baúl
twelve	doce
twenty	veinte
two	dos
ugly	feo/fea
uncle	el tío
van	la furgoneta
vegetables	las verduras
vehicles	los vehículos
to walk	andar
wardrobe	el armario
washbowl	el lavabo
water	el agua
wave	la ola
weather	el tiempo
whale	la ballena
wheelbarrow	la carretilla
wheelchair	la silla de ruedas
white	blanco/blanca
wind	el viento
window	la ventana
witch	la bruja
wood	el tablón
wreck	el naufragio
x-ray	la radiografía
x-ray machine	la máquina de rayos x
yacht	el yate
yellow	amarillo/amarilla
zebra crossing	el paso de cebra
zoo	el zoológico
zucchini	el calabacín

Colors – Los colores

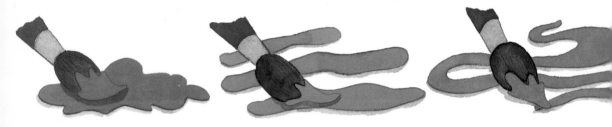

red
rojo/roja
ROH-hoh/ROH-hah

blue
azul
ah-SOOL

green
verde
VEHR-deh

yellow
amarillo/amarilla
ah-mah-REE-yoh/
ah-mah-REE-yah

black
negro/negra
NEH-groh/NEH-grah

orange
naranja
nah-RAHN-hah

white
blanco/blanca
48 BLAHN-koh/BLAHN-kah

purple
morado/morada
moh-RAH-doh/moh-RAH-dah

brown
marrón
mahr-ROHN

SPANISH-ENGLISH Picture Dictionary

Catherine Bruzzone and Louise Millar

Illustrations by Louise Comfort and Steph Dix
Spanish adviser: Diego Blasco Vázquez

digger
la excavadora
lah ex-kah-vah-DOH-rah

A simple, colorful picture dictionary
for young language learners. Here are over
350 useful words arranged in popular topics
including school, sports, park, beach,
house, street, farm, and wild animals.

boy
el niño
ehl NEEN-yo

fire engine
el camión de bomberos
ehl kah-mee-OHN deh bohm-BEH-ros

• Each Spanish word is clearly
illustrated for easy learning.

• A translation and simple pronunciation
guide is given for each word.

• Extra pages include numbers and colors.

orange
la naranja
lah nah-<u>RAHN</u>-hah

• Alphabetical Spanish-English and English-Spanish
word lists at the end of the book.

• A delightful first language book
for young children.

BARRON'S

ISBN: 978-0-7641-4661-9

9 780764 146619   50

$6.99   Canada $8.50
www.barronseduc.com